A Pear-Shaped World

poems by

Mary Strong Jackson

Finishing Line Press
Georgetown, Kentucky

A Pear-Shaped World

*For Josh and Kristy,
Nick and Mary, Katie and James,
Mya and Alex*

Copyright © 2025 by Mary Strong Jackson
ISBN 979-8-88838-969-0 First Edition
All rights reserved under International and Pan-American Copyright Conventions. No part of this book may be reproduced in any manner whatsoever without written permission from the publisher, except in the case of brief quotations embodied in critical articles and reviews.

ACKNOWLEDGMENTS

"The Backbone of Us", *El Palacio* magazine, Art, History, and Culture of the Southwest, Spring/Summer Issue, 2022, Santa Fe, NM

"What She Didn't Get" published as "Envy", *Chiaroscuro, An Anthology of Virtue and Vice*, 2021, Compiled by the Northern Colorado Writers

"Conversations after Breakfast" published as "Sobremesa", *From Other Tongues*, chapbook, 2017, Finishing Line Press

"Sestina" published as "She Carries", *Lummox*, Number 2, 2013 San Pedro, CA

Publisher: Leah Huete de Maines
Editor: Christen Kincaid
Cover Art and Design: Mary Strong Jackson
Author Photo: Steven Smith

Order online: www.finishinglinepress.com
also available on amazon.com

Author inquiries and mail orders:
Finishing Line Press
PO Box 1626
Georgetown, Kentucky 40324
USA

Contents

Untitled 1
The Backbone of Us 3
Not In America 5
We Are Carried 7
Slippery Moments 9
What I Would Untangle 11
Unlock 13
Cling 15
Caught Between a Cardboard Kaleidoscope 17
Who Gets the Boat? 19
Who 21
Waiting to Be Realized 24
Right as Rain 26
You're Joking 28
What She Didn't Get 30
Butterfly Time 32
Catching Breath During New Mexico Fires 34
Points 36
Manifest 38
Hungry Noise 40
The "It's Okay" Holiday 42
In Turn 44
The Edge of Now 46
Electing to Love the Silent Flow of Living Things 48
We are Souvenirs 50
Mutual Assured Restoration 52
Conversations after Breakfast 54
Verberations, Liberations, Chat GPT 56

Eve	58
Crossing the Border of Self	60
If the Tin Population Got Oiled	62
Life Turns on a Dime	64
Illness	66
JaNuaRy 2025 WhAt theHeLL? WhErE we GOin'? dO I NeeD mY CoAt?	68
Of These Lives	70
Grandma Didn't Die In the Corvair	73
Triumph	75
Catching Sight of One's Own Misery	77
Sestina	79
My Project 2025	82

Things have gone pear-shaped.
A British idiom when things, a plan, an idea have gone awry, failed, not working as hoped or expected.

Absolutely unmixed attention is prayer.
    Simone Weil

"Hope" is the thing with feathers—
That perches in the soul—
And sings the tune without the words—
And never stops—at all—
    Emily Dickinson

Without *hope* and *attention*, without a powerful and radical paradigm shift of our world systems moving away from the focus on wealth and productivity, we are going to fail as a species. Our lives may seem fine—grass greens with rain, sky remains blue, trees in every town. We don't miss insects not biting us, don't see vast numbers of animals in decline or forests retreating. Cognitive dissonance. Climate change is invisible except for those directly experiencing fires, floods, heat, and drought. With hope and attention, we can practice less harm with more passion.

Untitled

Can it be
there is a place
to be touched, stirred

as if with a spoon—creating an eddy
swirling open to the place love and sorrow
interlock—a place one must pass through
again and again

so we swirl lost in the eddy
catch our breath just in time many times

Standing on a pond reed
Rusty-orange dragonfly
What is our next move?

The Backbone of Us

Each vertebra nudges the next until all open their wings
across eons over pinon, pine, oak, cacti, and cottonwood
You feel it just under the skin of your backbone—swish, dip,
it radiates up the broad back of the plains to return
on the same line of the spine strong as woven silk
no matter the frayed bits.

My spine descended from Elder John Strong off the ship
called the Mary and John landing in 1630. His gentle turn
of head and shoulder, surreal flow of mind and spine—cogs
awakened repeating patterns taken time and again in the turn
of his head, to gather, to inhale with his eyes the brisk steps of men
and women striding across the land he was about to step onto.

Today, I enter the pool's bathhouse where two old women
talk of one's father entering Ellis Island at 2 years old, his
parents instructed *do not let the doctor remove your hat.*
He screamed and clutched his small cap
because something—I didn't catch in my eavesdropping—
some disease showed under the cap and the family would be
held   easy to forgive this escape from quarantine.

Each of our bony skulls connect with a series of small bones
forming the backbone having projections for articulation
able to speak of scars, skills, and inheritances to be shared
in bathhouses, slave quarters, mansions, then burned to ash,
spread, and inhaled by the living—chances to feel in this aching
ramrod of a country how to lift from bent knee,
how to swivel while supporting,
how to be an anchor for the entire body

With stick in soft dirt
She diagrams innocence
Horse bathes in twilight's dust

~~Not~~ In America

If the fascists come for me
I will hide my dog in the lining of my coat
and my cat in the other side
they will grow fat with pocket snacks,
the lining will tear, split, sunder
making trees do the same, clouds will slip
from the sky landing on hump-backed vultures.

Would I help a fascist into my claw-foot tub—
learn from where his pain or nonsense comes.
For now spring flower seeds emerge along
with morbid fascination—the new mode of impotence
as we watch the shaping of our states glue-gunned
together in sticky sad separateness.

Perhaps, eternal pain is something a country acclimates to,
meanwhile, save pillows for those who may inherit the earth,
watch your step across fracked land and state lines,
bring water, find shade. Wear 7-league boots, find a kind giant's
pocket to reside, just in case.

The World's Gone Pear-Shaped
Bites show on face and body
Sweet bits remain

We Are Carried

Fill a bucket with water, find rags,
remember instructions—use clean part of rag to wipe spills
from stones, or film remains. With gloved hand fill mortar
between, use small rocks as "chinking".

I like the word "chinking" reminds me of civilized dishes
at a tea party, but that's not me. I am not
tea cups, I am unmatched mugs, I am hard work.
I am daughter of a truck driver and a woman who carried.
I have learned to fit with chinking and chunking people.
My mother loved books. It made all the difference.
Even with gloves my hands know grit and search for broken pieces,
even with suffering between my shoulder blades,
my mother's love and books made all the difference.
I got here being carried.

Practice corner takes as long as childhood,
or peeling potatoes at a funeral dinner.
I thought I would like stonework, sturdy art,
solid labor. I thought I would stay married till I died,
but it was taking so long.

I moved to the long wall with new hope.
My practice perspective mortared
in my mind as I moved more stones
from trailer through gate onto ground.
We've all been carried. Thrown down or laid softly.
I place larger rocks on bottom rows, smaller ones near the top.
Children ride on shoulders, holding on to whiskers, bare chins or
necks.

I carry flat stones in my shirt like a bounty each one
finding place under the ledge where rounder rocks
nearly but not quite meet the wooden sill.
The stones begin to reveal desires about placement.
The work goes faster. Pleasure meets the pain
of living shifting up my back.
I remember parakeets carrying eggs from one laying box to another.

I, too, was carried.

Nurture a snail
Move around the city park
No tether needed

Slippery Moments

Just moments ago
a hood of heat hung
over the high desert
snakes sought deep holes
to ease the long hot muscles
under their skin
time to retract and fold fangs
for another day
Just moments ago
the full moon allowed a view
of the black puppy out to pee
unafraid near his people's door
he paused listened to his
non-curly cousins howling
in the near distance
Just moments ago
the hood of heat lifted
Dressed for dance, trees quivered.
Moments later, grooves deepened,
limbs let go their last shimmy of color
parts now pressed between pages
Just moments ago
unshelled peanuts outside the window
picked, shaken, taken in beaks of pinyon jays
packing away nuts with sun lighting blue wings
flying fast to hide hope in fallen leaves
Moments ago my father repeated,
"Don't let the screen door slam!"
Wood on wood, in and out, each kid letting go the door
ahh, for the chase, the urgency not to miss a moment
Just moments ago I say, *What is time, anymore*
You say that doesn't make sense *anymore?*
This moment—
shadows on adobe, cat asleep on a sill
just moments for dumplings to plump
in hot soup

Luck slips in and out
Cheer wakes with creamed coffee
Night pulls socks from feet

What I Would Untangle

I would untangle people who begin to look alike
sound alike who mush together in a tangled yawing sawing mass.

I would untangle the sad from their histories, the wrong-turn loops,
the jumps from too-high.

But I wouldn't, would I? What good are anecdotes minus aches,
twisting roads if unable to be lost, the good pain of numb fingers

warming, the sensing something palpable in the air when your mother
dies, or the rush of eye contact with an animal wilder than yourself?

We know after time together, one spooning foot will untangle from the other's.
Toes will touch the silk skin at the top of that foot a last time—

untanglings—knotted goodbyes

    —uncombed, remembered.

Ancient and New Math
Do not subtract! Add love!
Making a math of pluses

Unlock

If unlocked from your body—your constant,
your familiar—brimmed over with shoulds, oughts,
needs, musts, between ruminations and navel-gazing,
what would you do with a fissured and freed
bodiless self?

If untethered from your body might you travel
into a bird's hollow bones, or submerge in soil,
rise with warmth, feel the before, during, ultimate
burst of self into a many petaled big-headed sunflower?

Heard tell our grandchildren might live forever—
new limbs as needed, diseases cured.
Disregard taking turns—forget past instructions—
go on, eat ice cream in front of neighbor kids.
Become a land of slugs watching screens for centuries?

Seems better to transport a body—
land in Paris 1920ish feel slick and hungry
as a brush thirsty for paint, lie on Freud's velvet
burgundy couch, snicker at him until he calls
you hysterical, then tell him what you know
of the 2000s, feel him lie down next to you
on his overburdened couch in a nervous sweat
and chug water laced with cocaine.

Slip into Kathryn Hepburn's floaty-swishy-dresses
sail off a cliff into the song of a whale
where you will understand the leviathan's lyrics,
longer, deeper into the giant's vibrations
until you discern all indecipherable languages.

With the lock picked, the kernel, nucleus, marrow of you
might rock in time to the whole of life, no matter long or short.
Be a billiard ball freeing the triangle of those barely distinguishable
from yourself, or be the stick—
color yourself blue.

From bird's small throat
We ride each high and low note
Sensing her soarings

Cling

Justice clings to feelings—the way a particular sperm clings to an egg
determining a life of various shades, intro or extro-versions,
differing wills and depths to dive

Ice clings to cold until sun releases the hold and ice becomes
again a part of itself with whirlpools, currents, swirling others in its vortex
What will you cling to, what will you release

Somewhere snakes shed skins and a budding biologist
finds the see-through crinkly carriable skin once attached to snake,
carries it home with connections she senses but cannot name

Each of us—points in a pointillist painting, clinging to our spot
while a full moon hangs outside our points of view
and calls each to be closer

You think—it's crazy, but always has been and will be—
don't let the beans scorch, feed the woodstove,
cling to your someones

See how the moon looks at you—crazy, you are with the moon
Crazy because someday you won't be

Gratitudes exchanged
On Telegraph Avenue
Homeless man directs

Caught Between a Cardboard Kaleidoscope and Alternative Gene Splicing Events

Handheld dime store kaleidoscope thrilled
me once for a minute. Now I am here between
past and present exhaling in the belief
I will breathe tomorrow into more yesterdays

23,725 days equal peculiar episodes—riding
an elephant in Nebraska swaying atop a giant I had no right to ride
Day before last, I heard tales of gene-splicing
all the while knowing I am a middle knot of a connecting

loop from my parents' soft as sifted-flour-dust-bowl-dirt-days
seeping between their small toes to my grandchildren
who may opt to live forever as all disease composts away
Still, we put on pantaloons *one leg at a time*

perhaps a tinkered gene might make us born
with skin-deep clothing—no more clotheshorses—
for now we go on blighting, bejeweling and blessing

our bodies but can't reckon an end to weapon-building
clumsy us in all forward and backward sashays
building grace and calluses, hoping for blue guitar sounds
wafting across our picnics where we still
sit in backyards eating corn on the cob

some with whitened teeth and others who gnaw

Dangers are riddles
Try and fit under the wing
Of a half-grown eagle

Who Gets the Boat?

At the first flood, Noah's dog raced along
the bank of the almost always dry arroyo
water came quick as a hat trick making
a muddy river with waves visible from back doors.
How well-behaved must one be to board the boat?

Mud sucks around my rubber boots.
My left heel rises, my foot comes loose.
I am 8 years-old again half-afraid I'll lose
my boot in the muck but thrilled with the spirited-earth
sucking me still as water crosses Highway 502.

My dog loved our last impromptu river—
when she was good she was very very good,
but when she was bad she lunged and roared.
How many bites is dog allowed 1 or 2?
Water gushes through the berm onto

roots of the giant cottonwood—a sentinel,
watching all storms for 200 years.
Tree knows this place, knows this new heat
seeps deeper into her bare-of-bark places.
Flash floods sink around her roots,

mud pulls and loosens her hold.
Balding with age, her limbs drop wet bark
making dark walkways for skittering creatures.
Gnarls and burls big as buffalo heads
grow on her body and limbs, think elephant man,

think disease, think climate chaos.
One giant branch splits from her torso
other arms reach three stories.
Her leaves will dry and shimmer,
shading all beasts below until the day she falls,
unloosed like a foot in a boot, like a dog chasing
her last muddy river dream limbs moving in her sleep.

Just to measure warmth
She slipped her foot in his shoe
Love in wrinkled leather

Who

Who stepped on this ground before this foot
an hour ago, a day, a year

who spat, who shat along this path walking
with friend, spouse, child

who stroked this dog's ears yesterday
who kissed the muzzle of this dog's grandfather

who paddled the boat, the child,
the cream into butter

who wished he were dead, upon a star,
to go home

who worked the clay into beauty, the day into dark,
the gold in the mine

who stepped on a crack to break their mother's back,
out on you, across the line

who rained on your garden of dreams and bones,
on your wedding, on your parade

who dreamt the story, the bridge,
the possibilities

who bought the ring, the farm,
the dinner

who killed time, the bottle of rum,
his brother

who ruled the measure, the household,
the country

who raked the yard, the gravel,
you over the coals

who stroked the breast, the child's cheek,
a silky cat

who hungered for passion, for love,
for food

who shivered a minute, a hour,
to death

who bled, cried, pled, rejoiced, died on a cross, in a car, at a war
who whirled the dervish in love, hate, compassion, devotion

Coyote's red blush
Red-haired baby in cafe
Hungry memories

Waiting to Be Realized

I was young before my mother died
not that young but didn't know it
then my father died and I was not young anymore
and I knew it

their lives played out in front of me
as if I were the one dying and watching a life before my eyes
I see them in black and white
before they knew me
thin and sweet-faced
they knew hard times but not yet how hard

I remember them young
the scent of my father my mother's black eyelashes
and when I ease onto my own sheets
and open the book beside my bed
or when the sharp wind whips
my collar

I know they experienced the same
there is something in this knowing

The manatee winks
Thrusts her plain mermaid tail
Unlocks keyless hopes

Right as Rain

Long

      d
      r
      o
      p
      s

            of rain descend—

A Bundle of Thread say Germans.

Would you save your bundle for a rainy day?

Decline a rain check?
Pour bundles over yourself until

one
    more
        drop

makes the mineral springs in you run wild!

Until the rain of cats & dogs laps at your ankles

and you hear

Billie Holiday—

Don't threaten me with love, Baby. Let's just go walkin' in the rain.

Pillow flipping sleep
Out slips Pet through open door
Cottonwoods swish hellos

You're Joking

Accidents happen closest to home
one last orange blossom beer
and the stoop's last step

twists your ankle on what's supposed
to be the landing. Turns out home is for sloppy
punchlines, ill-timed quick jabs and sideway glances

that slip down the wrong-way
you forget the pause
the one that leaves the audience hanging

off start beginnings—you slept with who?
confused middles—maybe if you just bought a red convertible
quick endings—Grandma died at the casino in Deadwood?

You can't help but laugh as the oops-timed baby coos
up at you with eyes like stars

Creamed coffee breakfast
Mesa wears a snow doily
Dotting mountain life

What She Didn't Get

The dress with the red elephants
green vines, yellow flowers, and black stripes
with a slit up one leg and fringe where it counts.
The dress that got away
perfect for dancing on the plaza
and singing "I may be crazy".

The creamy caramel colored
French chair and ottoman—
it exhaled when sat in
like it needed her to breathe,
held her like a baby cloud
with nimbus arms and cumulus lap.

She nearly cried at the chair's comfort,
a too-high priced second-hand steal.
Once she got a chick dyed pink for Easter.
She walked in morning cold
to the feed store hoping new food
would save it.

Saw her friend's bird weeks later,
a living chicken, now just blue tips
at the end of white feathers.
It was the beginning
of knowing
some things are never yours.

Leonard Cohen sang
Dance me to the end of time
Desires remain

Butterfly Time

six and a half days
to make memories
to rub wings against another
to flatten your silhouette
then open your wings wide to what awaits

thousands of seconds
to sit with friends on orange and black Echinacea flowers
to lay your head into the gusts and become the morning's kite
a half day to carry the memories made
to settle in a bush that steals shadows without malice

to sit with your many legs
still as Buddha and feel breath pulse your wings
then listen to the sound of your six
feet clapping

Wading in ocean
Bell-bottoms wet to her knees
Small drop of human

Catching Breath During New Mexico Fires

A raven flies above me with its beak open
the air is smoky   seems best to hold one's breath
we share the flutter of change under wings and eyelids
what to do with smoke overhead or far away
with no way to puff it into rings as if at a party—

young with a new shag haircut, hoop earrings,
and a tan to turn one into a aged-speckled pup
one day in the future, a future landing too soon,
or at just the right time as is and shall be

forever and ever—wait—
this may end like the Jesus Freaks
told me under the Space Needle when I was 14
Last night the doves pretended to be owls

or the owls pretended to be doves
or was it me wanting to fly, hoot, and coo
in another language?
Where does one go to catch breaths?

Owls and doves are innocent and I am what?
Guilty when I accepted the plastic water bottle
as people around me dropped from heat
while waiting to see the Pope in 1993—

first time I'd seen water in bottles—I didn't know fish
would suffer   I wasn't in charge of knowing
now I know

First time I saw a woman portrayed as Jesus carrying
the cross on the field at Mile High Stadium
some men were angry

I knew she was perfect for the job

We're always circling
Or moving forward
in grand improvisations

Points

Suffering, what's the point
what's the sharp-edged knife point for
Not only the pointed-end pain
but the rough-edge for slow sawing
Creativity is the Solution said the t-shirt
he wore and believed
but imaginings come dark and dodgy, too

We believe spinning words, drool over sparkly bits
follow absurd hungers to try the largest hamburger in Crawford, Nebraska
said to be extinct but resurrected—evolution is a backward ride—

Crawford, where my aunt offered the image
of my mom, young, red lips, striking, dark haired girl-
woman standing by the bar with my future father,
slim, blue eyed, curly haired. Mom laughing,
sipping beer, not trying to crack the code of him—
who wants to in sweet moments of the unknown
—or know which of the many prayers would ease
pieces of her life

St. Anthony, St. Frances of Assisi, and don't forget
St. Jude—Patron Saint of Lost Causes able to come
through at the last moment
Trick is what does "lost cause" mean
when there's only facts of what is,
what unrolls, what evolves to mean a life

Holding struggles—those rocks in the gut times—
dispatches you into unfamiliar routes
you try shaking the map clean, try ripping
the entire book of maps in half until you laugh

We can straighten curly hair, or curl straight
but truth remains
try and stay on the same unbending road
you'll get curves, see dead raccoons—their black-gloved paws
questioning skyward—do you wince at the death, the wheeled cause,
or ignore and squint to keep from swerving

A rescued lizard
Spotted in house for days
Shares his bold tales

Manifest

Always been sharp tongues
able to slice through any argument
always been some *hotter than hell days*
but this heat makes one aware of every organ—

the one not playing on the street
the ones in your body wanting relief
while walking a Texas address in August
there's been days—your kid says he's not going to vomit
but does—not wanting to believe doesn't stop the purge,

ejection, eviction of us— *defenestrate   to throw out*
sounds like deforested as in karma
it didn't rain for years and then this summer
sunflowers popped in odd places—

happy faces turned upward in denial
or belief in reincarnation
everyone knows you can't hold the hand
of the dead for long

when we stand at the river with other thirsty
animals our throats too dry to growl
hoping for springs of eternal water
animal eyes won't blame the stewards

even without rights to land
we each could've claimed some bits
to mind where we stepped

Birds do not shun weeds
Most flowered heads are tasty
Eye of beholder

Hungry Noise

The air
thick with ambition
presses, kneads, churns,
Cortisol levels rise with oceans
as if readying to spear sharks
or herd a hundred heads over Zoom.

Atmospheres ring with targets and schemes,
but catch on weighty plates of despair until all exhaust
each day's sun into setting. Sun spirits itself up each morning,
shines on every past and present existence, every wondering ever wondered
Sun sees legacy's ways and wrenchings. It sets on words smothered
tight, not expressed, encased in each reflection ever reflected.

For centuries, seagulls circle and squall, coyotes,
too, continue their calls into the thickening air
of our searching selves snagging
on stirred systems rising above
the sweet and sour
sweat of us.

                    It's all for naught isn't it? To keep us occupied till death?

Lost in noisy clutter, failure to thrive
goes unnoticed by bejeweled nonsense. How could we be different
as we carry our spear now a phone, and lace our running boots to tackle
each day wrapped in its own skinned coat while seagulls circle
and screech in language few of us try to hear.
If we could decipher, might we sense

our airs of ambition, know we are
sanding our bones into dust
bit by bit until our knees
grind to silence then
will we know
the wisdom
of other
animals?

I met a recluse
Small hairy face looked at me
Emily? I asked

The "It's Okay" Holiday

What would you do Joe Cocker if I sang out of tune?
    I always do
Lower your reading glasses, touch your forehead
to mine, whisper, *It's okay?*

Not sure if the black puppy on my bed caused
the bear to enter my dreams with a claw
to her lips, saying, *Shhh, it's okay,*
while forests flame behind her.

Anyone can declare a holiday on this day
and any other—the way Christmas birthdays
celebrate in July—face someone and then
another someone with your eyes turned

to ON and say, *It's okay.*
These seconds, this minute, we are okay,
you are okay.

Say it to ailing trees, depressed monks, green bread,
to lovers who turn their backs, lost gypsies,
books caught in the rain,
to those out of tune.

Say it to leather couches with grandpa's
hair-oil stain, to cancer patients and their spouses,
to burnt pancakes asking for more butter,
more syrup.

Say it. All need to hear, *It's okay.*

What if hope is free
Turn over a rotting log
Be the lucky bear

In Turn

It is pleasant
to see a man turn—
pleasant as only moments grant
as on a winter's afternoon
when seconds of serendipitous light
and slivers of shadows languish
on an eave's icicle

The moment's gentle turn of head and shoulder
the surreal flow of mind and spine—cogs awakened—
repeat the patterns taken time and again
yet the mind
in this moment
allows for happenstance delights
subtle or sublime

It is pleasant to see a man
turn around to greet a woman
he knows or doesn't

Rain, Rain, Rain, Rain, Rain
Speak a word too many times
Its meaning drips down

The Edge of Now

I can't reconcile what can't be reconciled
don't know what to do with this acknowledgment—shape it
into a pendant to albatross my neck. No one is innocent but what is innocence
We dream and wake with plans, pursue impossible imaginings—
some succeeded—cleared forests, dammed rivers,
downed buffalos

From tiny tots pulling over water glasses, we continue reaching
no matter or because of the cold rush down our bodies, no
matter what exceeds our grasp, we reach for more

My friend tells of pulling the trundle bed out for her daughter's sleepover
first time since the little sister died who once slept there
they gasped at the shape of emptiness where the once small self
dreamed her dreams—shock and sorrow traversed
their bodies anew snagging memories
of sorrow and love entwined

Humans will be humans no matter the snag and pull
of collective memory. We each hold a ball of earth
our own mass to voodoo with sticks and spirits
poking pins in vulnerable spots and each other

I can't reconcile what can't be reconciled,
so I'll pull a chair to the edge of now,
remove the albatross from all
our necks—I'll try love,
silly and stale as this
sounds. Love,
for who and what
is now or has
been
I'll let this love snag
memories knowing
each entwines
with the other

Salt & Pepper parents
Once strangers in elevators
Blend peace and hardship

Electing to Love the Silent Flow of Living Things

After the election, heavy degrees of gray after casting of hope.
A silverfish swims across my bathroom floor—
Wingless insect silvery grey, fishlike, the tile, its ocean.
Without fins following its own future.
Its own silent flow.

The earnest pup predicts we'll play. Knows words, knows love,
knows the silent arc of airborne ball.
Tabby arrives in living color—shades of rocks, wet-bark browns,
Inner ears—tulip pink, eyes—green of flower stem.
Half-grown chicks greet me for passage of greens, hand to beak.
They cock heads as I do mine—we have begun to know each other
In these quotidian days, quaint except the disquietude.
The malaise, the dis-ease of us.

When true cold comes, I will break pond ice for fish
Who go deeper, survive winter by calming their bodies.

After the election, I straighten friends' artwork,
Move boxes of books, slipping into them, reading bits,
Until my body says *move,* then I pull up old carpet they've been boxed upon
While talking with each other of history's whippings, of odd love
For barrel and bullet, greed of human hungers even if a full belly.
Suffering souls no matter upon whose side one sits.

Morning after, I backstroke through my creamy
Coffee in a small cup of a world, but know I live in this big, loud land.
I pull the Wonder Woman t-shirt over my head, the one I bought my daughter
Years ago, and pull on baggy flared jeans, reminding of ones worn
Wading in the ocean, age 14, with a boy named Dusty.
Wavy sounds of words as water swished over wet knees.

He spoke of factory work assembling meals for boy soldiers—
The speed, the sounds of boxed food—tasteless he said.
Day after election—sudden dehydration, imbalance of fluid hope.
Dry scorching fears.

Two loud ravens croak
Talking how to build nests
Listen up for tips

We are Souvenirs

She will hand me a piece of glacier—straight from her cooler—
a baby iceberg. I like the word "calving"
the way it comes with noise—mother cow bellowing,
a cracking sound, a plunge of ice in water
loosed from its mother.

She will ask, "Will you keep it cold? Not use it for lemonade?"
Once someone placed a piece of concrete in my hand—
calved, you might say, from the Berlin Wall.

Souvenirs from places torn down or disappeared. Hunt and gather,
hunt and gather if only we knew, or listened, and 12-stepped
away from our addictions.

Odd animals, us. Always wanting more. Chewing off
good parts of self for years and years until melted
they cannot renew. For now, no rewinds, just clocks inside
ourselves with flashes of dates—Mt. St. Helen's erupted on my
birthday.
I may be alive to know when the sea swallows Florida,
the morning the first climate refugee knocks.

Nothing to lose, but a freezer-burned bit
of glacier and an ugly piece of wall.

Baby chicks huddle
Eleven in a straw bed
One peeps loudest

Mutual Assured Restoration

A doctrine of non-military strategy
a security policy of the people
a full-scale use of non-injurious weapons on all sides
would cause definite life
of both promoters and receivers
and welcome second attacks of transformation
from arrested adolescence

This theory is not based on deterrence
which wield threats, instead employs
the use of different arms—brotherly,
sisterly ones able to wrap and hold others—
as incentive to initiate mutual assured restoration

Goat-head thorns spread arms
Lizards liven flower beds
Black Mesa sees all

Conversations after Breakfast

Pinon coffee pours into cups
a serum for truth or near truths
should a life story be told only once
to keep it honest—no matter
someone reminds from the "Queen" to imagine
6 impossible things before breakfast
What have you dreamed
I dreamed the baby girl's first words
came while sitting on my bed
she looked into my eyes and said, "steel, stone, bone"
solid words from rosebud lips
        contradictions   contraindications   coincidences
existing in more than one world in more than one way
letting go of commands, directives and yeah-buts
Ahh, the impossible possibilities we speak this day after breakfast
the taste of the eyes around the table make me lick my lips
I might swallow a whole lake if sipped daily
every cross or uncross of arms feels familiar
to each hair on my skin
Is it my eyes or shadows blending space between
eyes, speckled arms and four-chambered hearts
Are the two dogs and one cat already here at this breakfast
or signs to come based on the configuration of potted plants
and assorted gatherings on the window sill
once I brought home the spine of an antelope carcass
one might get stiffer-backed as she grows old
or slip into other bodies more easily than ever
After Huevos Rancheros there's an easing into self—
a newborn curling still present in the awakened
before the hardness of noon and the resolve of night

After a long rain
Pay a dime to see Sam
swallow gutter's nightcrawlers

Verberations, Liberations, Chat GPT

Reverberation holds still the verb in it.
Much to know of a word's origin—whose lips bounced
a certain sound into whose mind and somewhere, sometime
a meaning for an object, thought, feeling became a word?

I don't know how my heart reverberates towards yours,
yours messages another's, that heart stirs more
and so on making a steady beating of billions
of reverberations all drumming beats, warming some, breaking others.

Do I want things and people to be more than something
with heart if the what of them is that they are the thing they are?
We vibrate in ways unknown to each other, which may translate
into our wanting *seen*. This may be unraveled one day
into each having a clear vision of every other,

but where would awkward go?

Those moments not knowing what to say or where to stand,
how to still one's heart, and if not seeing in the other's face
and body the harboring of desires, dreads, fires, and fears
we would be left without the edgy bits, the dodgy, gawky,

ticklish unquiet to scratch, unleashing the red, raw
itches of us. Left without senses of this sort to sort out,
which is odd asking to be seen when being seen means a peeling
of the skin with its tuned-up insights, and reverberations—it would mean

removing the body's verb no matter active or passive—
not allowing the skin to reflect the reverberating heart.

Too many questions
Sluice at us from open gates
Flood our plains

Eve

Eve kept analyzing
The whole god-damned situation
Until her rib bones ached

She took one out
Began to carve and carve
She worked her knife

Pressing her body weight
With each stroke
A rhythm began

The rib bone grew bigger bigger
And became a canoe
Big enough for Eve to get inside

Embrace the cold jump
An ancient woman backstrokes
Raw salty bare-skinned

Crossing the Border of Self

we are at our best when things are the worst

Must we have *"The Worst"* to whip us into plain uncluttered goodwill—
we've tied a bungee cord to earth to see how close we get to the edge.
What if the cord is too long, or it's a bounceless bungee?
While we wait for the fall, we cavort in play-offs with fascism.

The richer we become, dressed in fashionable concertina wire—
with more things stuffed with things—cheese-stuffed pizza crust,
luxury dinghies on yachts, one house able to fit into your other house.
We build fortresses around our homes, keep classics from children,
take the Christ out of Christian. Rich in AR-15s—someday
we'll park personal tanks outside schools, and ponder why more children
die by violence.

There remain riches of tiny lizards doing push-ups on stones warmed by the
sun, buffalo scratching majestic heads on cottonwoods near the Platte River,
acrobatic squirrels, and whales' songs.

Seems crossing the border of self is in order—feed howling dogs inside
ourselves, open stuck gates, disperse our guards with their false forebodings,
cross the border of self, find the peaceful territories of each other,
shed excess, try the art of sacrifice—
we might survive.

Or, put on suits of armor, grip our swords, wait for the end
we will be trapped behind borders of self.

It will be hot.

Who is welcome here
Open doors slammed hard and fast
Sad skies wept large drops

If the Tin Population Got Oiled

The loaded, slippery raindrop—a pause before falling,
a pause before your finger pushed
Send—and Orbison's lyrics "Fading Away",
written without his protective sunglasses,
lit my screen   then you died

Once, it was explained what made Cassevetes' films great
—in life, real exchanges are few. He gifted 90 minutes
of true talk in films, relevant—as gloves in winter,
as raindrop-tears sliding down a face on the bus

But could we endure more than seconds of palpable unarguable
feelings—each saying what's not been said
might we perish in the heat of sincere truths,
the unsheathing of naked nerves

held since childhood's imprint of imitations,
cramped in our gut's ancient archives,
if unloosed—thunderstorms across lands—
vast, quaking, burgeoning fearless
feelings unearthed from one to another to another

Our drumming hearts outing from unbuttoned selves,
lighting every curled cochlear
Every illness ever ailed leaving bodies
rocking and being rocked

Dead folks crowd my mood
Old dog stares with knowing eyes
January's ice stays on

Life Turns on a Dime

Black Kitty rose one morning
and I with her—our usual start—
the way she would say, "water"
in meow words and I would top her off.

This morning, she didn't demand when I turned
the faucet handle. Instead, her nose bumped
against furniture, one chair then another.
Kitty rose one morning, landed on a turning dime
and was blind.

But she never cared for money.
Found her way upstairs to lie in the sunny windowsill,
located her litter box, her food and water.
Kitty carried on while the rest of us
polished rocks, coveted pearls,

and watched dances from those with tender toes
turning on dimes while others
rested in comfortable shoes.

Kitty found her way onto warm chests to lie upon.
Did she care she'd outlived two dogs, gave
up catching mice and tiny lizards?
I've heard cats have walnut-sized brains.
How not to grieve for all those lives turning on dimes
dispersed every hour, every day

when we know how that dime
feels in our sweaty palm?

Walk all twisty routes
Decline a few passageways
Walk unmarked byways

Illness

for my children

If labeled with a name, objects, creations, conjectures
are limited in all they could become
held by permanent boundaries—framed rivers unable to flow

I want to use the name Suture, as in closure, or Aid as in healing
I have no power to change the name of illnesses
better known as disorders, attacks, knock-down-drag-outs

I want to take illness to court, change its name,
issue restraining orders, put a tight enclosure around
its chronic nature and voodoo abilities,

but if I fight what's inside my adult children's bodies,
it makes me an enemy of a part of them
How to beckon what saddens, frightens, angers

What charmed monikers might soothe ailments—
make sickness sleep forever never to be kissed awake

I'll offer names with wings
—Owl, Wren, Eagle, Raven, Hawk

Arise in sloth-time
Linger with toad in flowers
Take a baboon breath

**JaNuaRy 2025 WhAt theHeLL? WhErE we GOin'?
dO I NeeD mY CoAt?**

I was a prairie pup in green-checked jacket
sitting on the roof of a backyard shed
watching the drive-in movie screen blocks away
no sound reaching us
we made up words mouthed by actors
the neighbor kid hogging his Etch-a-Sketch
only lets me shake it clear

Yeah but, Now? in this curious
goddess of a world—I turn the 8-ball
over   it says "I cannot predict" "try again"
The odds of you being born is 1 in 400 trillion
What lucky lottery winners we are

Born to sit across from each other
taking all for granted at a table made from a tree
whose odds of growing tall enough
to be wanted by lottery winners was too great—
born to be cut

some would say the same for humans
but who does the slicing
we all want a place to put our plate

The funniest man I didn't know
had obsessive compulsive disorder
making him touch every picture in the hallway
put out his tongue and lick the air
to the right, to the left

scientists can rid our DNA of these
air lickers and erase the funniest man
I wouldn't know in my future

which is getting shorter by the way
with little time to understand
where we're going and if I need my coat

Three muddied chickens
Changed flat tires in white suits
Rain-spattered road

Of These Lives

After W.S. Merwin's "One of the Lives"

If my grandfather had not found France a dirty country when stationed
there in WWII he might have had more lust for travel and too

if he'd not been stout and strong with the makings of a blacksmith
and work waiting in Nebraska where his twelve brothers and sisters

lived and where the one named Lottie who did not want the death
penalty for a killer who murdered her daughter because it would not

bring her child back and this making an impression on my mother
towards common sense except in the fact of her father's gruffness

causing her to marry a man charm and blue eyes who sang
in the bars and whose greed for a good time was full-time and lacking

what one might call good judgment and she said once it was two weeks
after they wed at age nineteen she knew he was not the man she thought

and if only her mother had not believed mom too young to accept an art
scholarship in Michigan she may not have spent as much time on her knees

praying or had to work through 6 pregnancies needing cigarettes to relieve
stress but blackening her lungs though she may not have created paintings

in her 50s after the long search for the colors of harmony which brings calm
to viewers of her art. Mother believed I would have stayed married to my

good man of many years if I had not watched her remain in a flawed
relationship plus she accepted fault easily for any wrongs her children

might have done and she did not judge her daughter's choices
and considered there may be more to marriage than sobriety and steady

work and a church's decree and if I'd stayed I would not have found
my places to labor and loiter would not have tripped where I needed

to fall and would not have seen the reflection of ravens in another's eyes
or realized she stayed to become who she was and knew I had to leave

for the same reason but she did not know whatever good I carried
from Nebraska were the parts of her I held inside

Squat with chickens
Cocked heads side-eyed looks
Repetition breeds familiars

Grandma Didn't Die In the Corvair

She waited till her black Irish brows grayed
after she'd wandered town looking for tiny girls
she thought were lost
stopping at the man who sold cars to inquire about the girls

He had no arms
but a finger grew from the place his arms
should be—a thalidomide baby grandmother said
and I imagined this man

holding girls so tiny he curled one finger
around their waists and when he turned his head
he was eye to eye with them
and when he looked forward they stared

at the moles on his neck
hoping he wouldn't drop them
Now grandma seems like a dream offering
gingersnaps and workbooks to do while my tonsils shrink

Wait long enough and dead people
are dreams you can't quite grasp
but remember when something in the day reminds—
someone says icebox instead of fridge

Then your mother is old and dies
and you remember two women getting old
then they die though they once
ate brownies and tied their shoes
in the wind

Step into winter
snake-like hose gathered
Its sunned softness rolled

Triumph

Adding a new line to your resume
stating you taught a child to make soup
even if that child is yourself
the invitation of herbs
the dropping into liquid

The easing out of trying too hard
The resting into the hammock
of your own skin

Subtle sounds signal
Dance is familiar it's true
Right foot first or left?

Catching Sight of One's Own Misery

She'd caught sight of it
in shadows like a mouse
along the baseboards

but this wanted her to see
and scurried less
seemed larger than before
She felt an unveiling coming
a reckoning
so she held a heavy blanket
one moonlit night and caught it

It had body and weight
afraid to uncover it
but feeling she must
she laid the heavy thing on the bed
unwrapped it at a snail's speed
making her bones ache with effort
felt a clawing under her skin

Once unveiled
it spelled out words
each letter carved
from parts of her
soot, grime, boils,
and blood
road rash and ringworms

She folded the blanket
around it
held it against her
offered warm tea
and rubbed it with oil
to soften each part that protruded

then whispered as she rocked it, *Mistakes can be rounded away from sharpness. There will be no more dark scurrying.*

At Easter Egg Hunt
Came upon a one-eyed frog
The green pirate

Sestina

She considers putting down the light,
pulling a blanket of bark over her face
easing into this good night
but she carries on. To carry means to live.
A million eggs she carries in her tiny womb purse,
above her womb, a leather bag of heart she fills, carries.

She lifts with her back, she lifts with her legs, she carries
sums and subtractions. She lifts them to the light
until need and doubt shape and purse
her lips, bag her eyes, and rope the muscles in her face.
Knots on knots to untie, iron, square this life
into the orange-blue sunset on tap for such nights.

She carries the man asleep on the sofa into the night.
She learned young to haul and pull, tote and carry.
It's what women do, bring others to life,
seek darkness to poke holes where light
finds a way, so all know which way to face
for the most sun and what to pack in each day's purse.

One purse carries every-occasion tools, another purse
tissues of grief. For blood-red styles on cool nights,
she chooses wine with kangaroo bodies and kangaroo faces,
and in her pouch's darkest caves she carries
White Clay, Nebraska passed out in the light
and Juarez, Mexico's tiny hands begging to live.

Some days she longs to carry nothing, to live
without the weight of a raindrop on her purse
to live without a purse, carry only a headlight
used to spill a stream of light in the blackest night
but no matter, she would find a snail to carry,
to nurture, to ask if too much light shone in its little face.

If carrying one's home on the back strains the face,
if a knowing hook for your coat doesn't make a life,
she considers dropping house and all she carries
taking only what she pours into her purse
sliding away with a small light into the night
leaving all that scurry in her lightbeam.

Her heavy purse spills into the laps of life
bits of living collages reflect her face, she lowers the light
and draws into the night owning all she carries.

Barefeet warmed by sun
Walking into the world's winds
Palpable presence

My Project 2025

Loving hard comes to mind which also includes loving soft
Love the way my 1 hand holds the other when injured—try to be like my hands

I will not waste my unease or rest in disquietude but seek liminal spaces—as words hang for seconds between your lips and my ears
One cannot speak on the inhale—I'll love the pause between inhale—(time to listen) and exhale   try to note tiniestdistance betweensyllables

I will remember as needed
the space of joy between the toddler and the bed he landed upon

and love crooked as a tooth overstepping its bounds, love straight, love jagged, love raw

I'll note the hesitancy of anything I am about to bite onto or into
Love my exhaustion and dirt under nails

Imagine gills, dive 10,000 leagues deep into the sea of others to see who I am
Love the way Samuel Beckett gave Andre the Giant rides to school for years
Try to be as brave in truth as Bishop Mariann Edgar Budde, and loyal and wild as Queegueg without killing whales

Love enough—ponder what that means

use often the words *relish* and *nurture* and *suture* for their sounds (and meaning)

reckon what being *human* is or if I might rather be like the clawed, hairy, snouted, or fanged animal knowing how to live my *one and only life*

Cupping curves of ocean
Whispering watery words
Wonderings about wonder

Mary Strong Jackson's beginnings were formed between wooden church kneelers and bar stools. Born to an Irish mother who read from a steady stack of library books, and a truck driver father who cared little for the written word. She comes from tornadoes, buffalo wallows, ruby and topaz sunsets of Western Nebraska. Raised in Nebraska, Mary also spent short but important periods in Washington and Oregon. As a social worker, she was employed in Nebraska, New Mexico, and England. Before getting her bachelor's degree in social work and an M.ED, she began writing poetry at her kitchen table as a stay-at-home mother of three. Poetry transformed mundane daily chores into validations of her life. As a social worker her career focused on adults, foster children, and their parents with diagnoses of mental illness. She facilitated a poetry and writing group for 4 years at The Life Link Santa Fe Clubhouse and Wellness Center, a psycho-social rehabilitation facility for adults with mental illness and/or substance abuse. Mary supervised staff and all other programs at this facility. As a poet and a social worker, her desire to give voice to those with mental illness, resulted in a collaboration with clients in the creation of *Singing Under Water*, a book of poetry and prose. Mary's chapbook titles are *Dreaming in Grief, From Other Tongues, The Never-Ending Poem by the Poets of Everything, Witnesses, No Buried Dogs, Between Door and Frame,* and *Clippings*. In 2005, Mary was chosen to participate in a Nebraska Educational Television program featuring United States Poet Laureate, Ted Kooser. Mary resides in New Mexico near Otowi Bridge on the Rio Grande.

www.ingramcontent.com/pod-product-compliance
Lightning Source LLC
Chambersburg PA
CBHW030054170426
43197CB00010B/1516